The Sermon on the Mount

Colouring Book

The Soothing, Simple to Colour Words of Christ

Matthew 5: King James Bible Verses

Copyright © Magdalene Press 2016

ISBN 978-1-77335-089-9

No part of this publication may be reproduced, stored in a retrieval system, or transmitted in any form or by any means, electronic, mechanical, photocopying, recording or otherwise without written permission of the publisher.

Magdalene Press, December 2016

Matthew 5

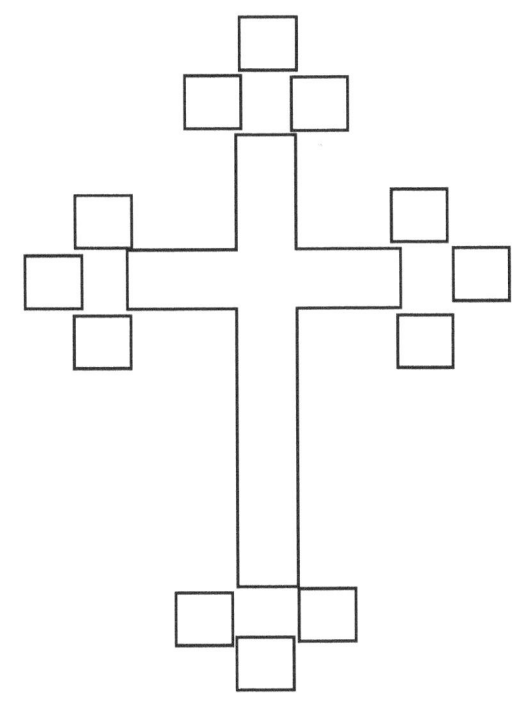

1

And seeing the multitudes, he went up into a mountain: and when he was set, his disciples came unto him:

2 And he opened his mouth, and taught them, saying,

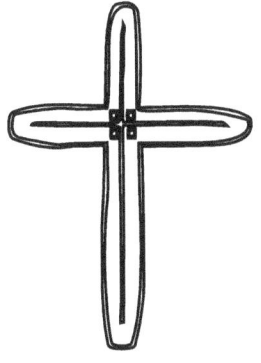

3

Blessed are the poor in spirit: for theirs is the kingdom of heaven.

4

lessed are they that mourn: for they shall be comforted.

5

Blessed are the meek: for they shall inherit the earth.

6 Blessed are they which do hunger and thirst after righteousness: for they shall be filled.

7

Blessed are the merciful: for they shall obtain mercy.

8

Blessed are the pure in heart: for they shall see God.

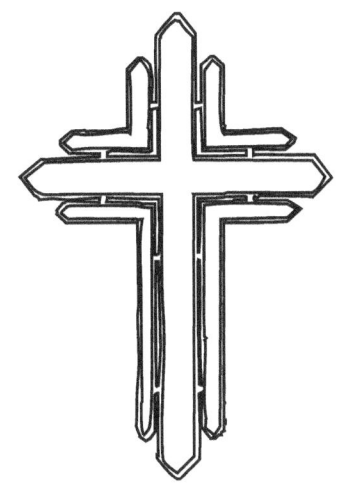

9 Blessed are the peace-makers: for they shall be called the children of God.

10 Blessed are they which are persecuted for righteousness' sake: for theirs is the kingdom of heaven.

11 Blessed are ye, when men shall revile you, and persecute you, and shall say all manner of evil

against you falsely, for my sake.

12 Rejoice, and be exceeding glad: for great is your reward in heaven: for so persecuted they

the prophets which were before you.

13 Ye are the salt of the earth: but if the salt have lost his savour, wherewith shall it be salted? it is

thenceforth good for nothing, but to be cast out, and to be trodden under foot of men.

14 Ye are the light of the world. A city that is set on an hill cannot be hid.

15 Neither do men light a candle, and put it under a bushel, but on a candlestick; and

it giveth light
unto all that are
in the house.

16

Let your light so shine before men, that they may see your good works, and glorify your Father which is in heaven.

17 Think not that I am come to destroy the law, or the prophets: I am not come to destroy, but to fulfil.

18

For verily I say unto you, Till heaven and earth pass, one jot or one tittle shall in no wise pass

from the law, till all be fulfilled.

19 Whosoever therefore shall break one of these least commandments, and shall teach

men so, he shall be called the least in the kingdom of heaven: but whosoever shall do and teach them, the same shall be called great in the kingdom of heaven.

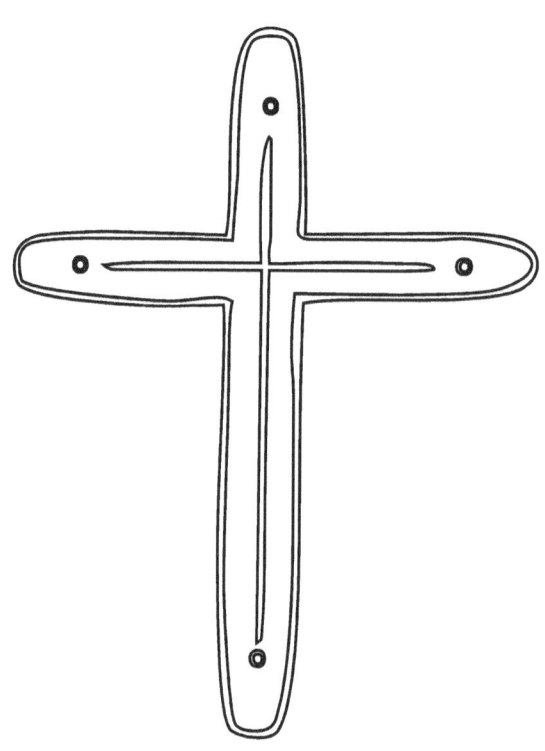

20 For I say unto you, That except your righteousnes s shall exceed the righteous-ness of the

scribes and Pharisees, ye shall in no case enter into the kingdom of heaven.

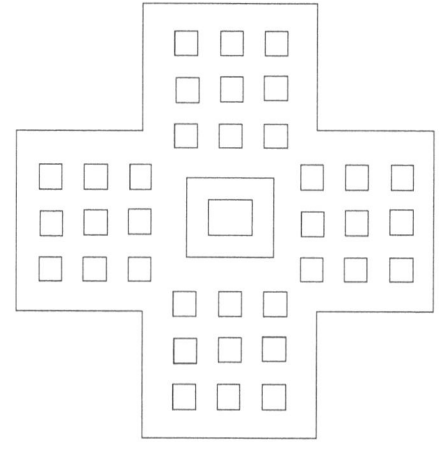

21 Ye have heard that it was said of them of old time, Thou shalt not kill; and whosoever shall

kill shall be in danger of the judgment:

22

But I say unto you, That whosoever is angry with his brother without a cause shall be in danger of the judgment: and whosoever shall say to his brother, Raca, shall be in danger of the council: but whosoever shall say, Thou fool, shall be in danger of hell fire.

23 Therefore if thou bring thy gift to the altar, and there rememberest that thy brother hath ought against thee;

24

Leave there thy gift before the altar, and go thy way; first be reconciled to thy brother, and then come and offer thy gift.

25

Agree with thine adversary quickly, whiles thou art in the way with him; lest at any time the adversary deliver thee to the judge, and the judge deliver thee to the officer, and thou be cast into prison.

26

Verily I say unto thee, Thou shalt by no means come out thence, till thou hast paid the uttermost farthing.

27 Ye have heard that it was said by them of old time, Thou shalt not commit adultery:

28 **B**ut I say unto you, That whosoever looketh on a woman to lust after her hath

committed adultery with her already in his heart.

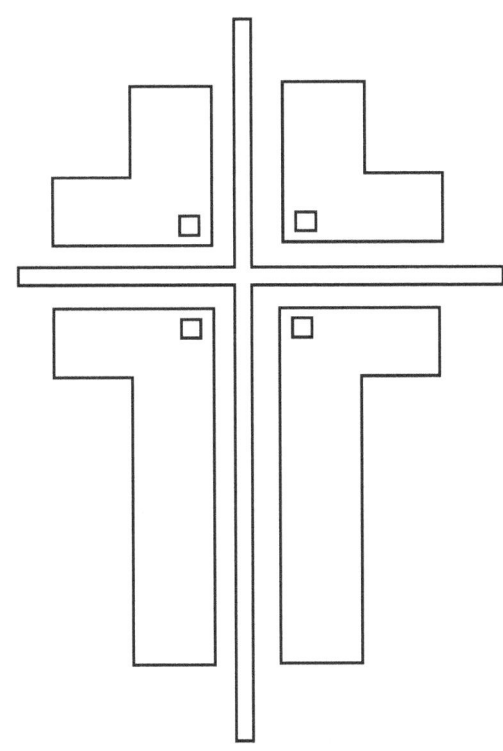

29 And if thy right eye offend thee, pluck it out, and cast it from thee: for it is profitable for

thee that one of thy members should perish, and not that thy whole body should be cast into hell.

30 And if thy right hand offend thee, cut it off, and cast it from thee: for it is profitable for

thee that one of thy members should perish, and not that thy whole body should be cast into hell.

31 It hath been said, Whosoever shall put away his wife, let him give her a writing of divorcement:

32 But I say unto you, That whosoever shall put away his wife, saving for the cause of

fornication, causeth her to commit adultery: and whosoever shall marry her that is divorced committeth adultery.

33

Again, ye have heard that it hath been said by them of old time, Thou shalt not forswear thyself, but shalt perform unto the Lord thine oaths:

34 But I say unto you, Swear not at all; neither by heaven; for it is God's throne:

35

Nor by the earth; for it is his footstool: neither by Jerusalem; for it is the city of the great King.

36

Neither shalt thou swear by thy head, because thou canst not make one hair white or black.

37 But let your communication be, Yea, yea; Nay, nay: for whatsoever is more than these cometh of evil.

38 Ye have heard that it hath been said, An eye for an eye, and a tooth for a tooth:

39 **B**ut I say unto you, That ye resist not evil: but whosoever shall smite thee on thy right

cheek, turn to him the other also.

40 And if any man will sue thee at the law, and take away thy coat, let him have thy cloak also.

41

And whosoever shall compel thee to go a mile, go with him twain.

42

Give to him that asketh thee, and from him that would borrow of thee turn not thou away.

43

Ye have heard that it hath been said, Thou shalt love thy neighbour, and hate thine enemy.

44 But I say unto you, Love your enemies, bless them that curse you, do good to them that hate

you, and pray for them which despitefully use you, and persecute you;

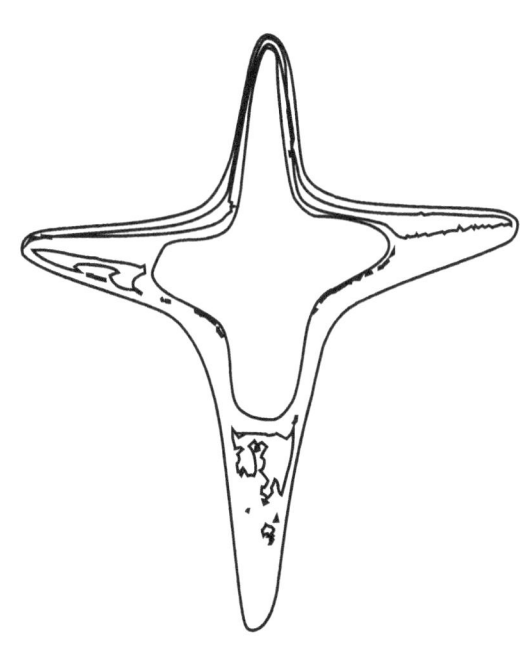

45 That ye may be the children of your Father which is in heaven: for he maketh his sun

to rise on the evil and on the good, and sendeth rain on the just and on the unjust.

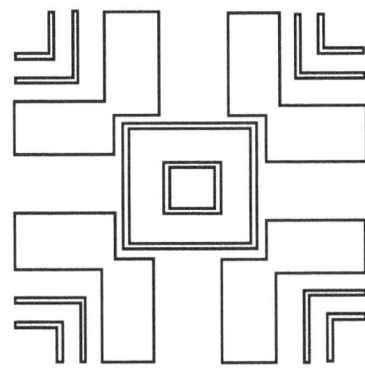

46

For if ye love them which love you, what reward have ye? do not even the publicans the same?

47 And if ye salute your brethren only, what do ye more than others? do not even the publicans so?

48 Be ye therefore perfect, even as your Father which is in heaven is perfect.

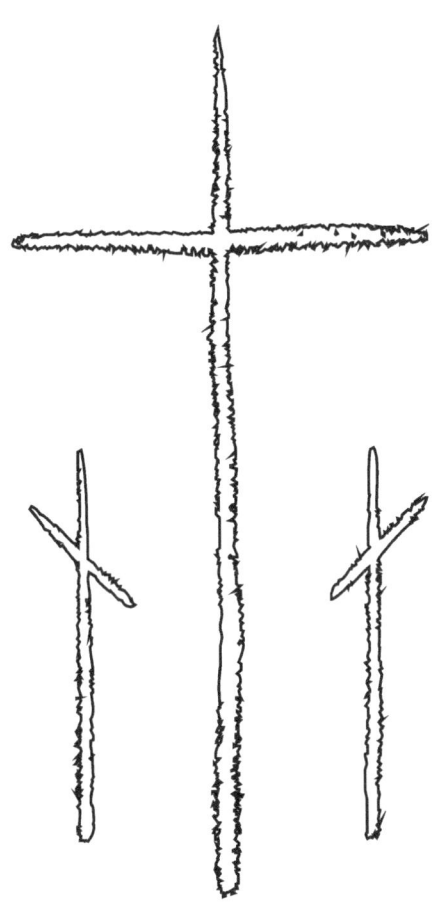

www.ingramcontent.com/pod-product-compliance
Lightning Source LLC
Chambersburg PA
CBHW051258110526
44589CB00025B/2872